Uncovering
Wild at Heart

Journey Into the Therapeutic Gospel

FHI
BOOKS
Power in Reality

"See to it that no one takes you captive through philosophy and empty deception, according to the tradition of men, according to the elementary principles of the world, rather than according to Christ."

Colossians 2:8, NASB

Tom Griner

Author of *Wounded Continent*

Uncovering
Wild at Heart

Journey Into the Therapeutic Gospel

A Teaching Analysis of John Eldredge's
Best-selling Book *Wild at Heart*

Uncovering Wild at Heart
A Journey into the Therapeutic Gospel

ISBN 0967750814

Library of Congress #2006900406

FHI
BOOKS
Power in Reality
P.O. Box 846
Bishop, CA 93515
USA

tcgriner@juno.com

Printed in the United States of America

For information about other materials, visit our website:
www.tomgriner.com

Cover photo by Arunan Manivannan

To all of those who love the truth.

TABLE OF CONTENTS

······································

PREFACE

······································

As I have taken the time to look closely at the presuppositions and doctrine presented in John Eldredge's *Wild at Heart*,[1] I have done so with no other motive than a concern for the people of God and a love for truth.

I don't question the sincerity of John Eldredge, but as you shall see, I sincerely question his ability to rightly divide the word of truth. What he has written may be a best-seller, but it is also a Trojan Horse filled with seeds of deception. I know this may sound harsh and unkind, but his book is not just a biblical opinion that is as valid as any other. It is a message that attacks the nature of the gospel of the Bible at its core, changing it into another gospel—a therapeutic gospel. And if you will follow me through a careful examination of what is being said here in the light of the Scripture, you will see exactly what I am talking about.

Though Eldredge might place this review in the class of what he calls the "self-appointed doctrine police" (a Pharisee), my confrontation with his teaching is simply an effort to, "contend earnestly for the faith which was once for all delivered to the saints" (Jude 3). And as I have done so, I have given very little effort in trying to appear like this is some kind of fair and balanced critique. I mean I have not tried to balance the bad by finding some good thing to report on. The reason being, the issues are so serious and grievous that any good is completely washed out by the bad. There can be no compromise with what would erode sound doctrine and the centrality of Christ.

I know that for some the words *sound doctrine* have a rather metallic ring, stale and static, something seemingly irrelevant to the church of the 21st century. Nevertheless, the apostle Paul values the term, admonishing, " . . . watch your life and doctrine closely. Persevere in them, because if you do, you will save both yourself and your hearers" (1 Timothy 4:15-16).

I have received several letters from young men who have made Paul's words very meaningful to me. In response to this critique, they have written, in no uncertain terms, that no matter what I say, they know *Wild at Heart* is true because of how it makes them feel. I would in no way discount what help a person may have received from this book, but I would still say, its popularity is not that it is true, rather that it scratches an itch; and because it does it so well, it is assumed to be true. As the song goes, "If it feels so right, how can it be wrong?"

But the itch is not about what is biblically sound and moral, nor is it about righteous obedience to the Word of God. It is about something supposedly much more sublime; a man's heart passion (feelings) freed from the old stereotypes of duty and responsibility (morals). It is about desire; the desire for adventure, battle, and a golden-haired woman.

It is these lively masculine themes that John Eldredge uses to draw men to sit with him on his *Wild at Heart* therapy couch where he applies his therapeutic gospel. And because this work is just one more in a platoon of therapeutic books that is resetting the mindset of the church, its popularity is guaranteed. As we shall see, *Wild at Heart* is a psychological gospel targeting a psychologized church that has itching ears.

Increasingly, Christians are living their lives by the way they personally feel in their hearts and consciences. These Christians have this encroaching thought that if it feels true, it must be true. This, though, is nothing more than the "cooking down" affect of living in a relativistic and therapeutic culture. Christianity in the 21st century is becoming increasingly "subjectified" and "inward." Christians feel a *disconnect* with the external and objective written Word of God, especially with its call to moral living (Titus 2). But with no solid tether to biblical teaching, the lives of many Christians are being shaped by their own self-centeredness and the influence of the hidden cultural assumptions in which we all live (what feels right, looks right, what benefits me, what feels true).

When the "'inward feeling of things" becomes the guide for Christian life and practice, deception is immanent. Then everything relates to the benefit of the person and how it makes them feel. When they do come to the Bible (or any book/ message/teaching), they often come to "me and the Bible" with an emphasis on me.

In response to this feeling-orientated Christian culture, the producers of much of what is hitting the book shelves and being taught in churches is increasingly anecdotal, softened, and therapeutic. They are catering to the new orientation by feeding it with "'touchy-feely" content, content designed and tailored for the emotions and feelings of the believer. Why? Because it is popular and sells. The result is Christianity void of substance, impact, and authority, and people who have lives built on answering the question, "how does it feel?"

This is the day Paul warned Timothy to be on the look out for:

> "For the time will come when men will not put up with sound doctrine. Instead, to suit their own desires, they will gather around them a great number of teachers to say what their itching ears want to hear. They will turn their ears away from the truth and turn aside to myths." (2 Timothy 4:3-4)

This was no small thing to Paul. He went to great lengths to encourage his disciples to give careful attention to doctrine. In fact, soundness of doctrine, faith, and speech is a basic concern in his Pastoral Letters (1, 2 Timothy; Titus). You might say Paul was encouraging them to be *doctrine police.*

So, I am compelled to shine the light of Scripture on *Wild at Heart,* in the hopes that some will be turned from its misguided influence. As you read this critique, I pray that you would be encouraged and instructed in a greater view of what it means to have a Christ-centered gospel and sound doctrine.

Introduction

....

THE REASONS WHY

....

I am sure John Eldredge wants to help men, and in this very cleverly written book, he brings his best prescription for the restoration of the wounded masculine soul. The book has created a buzz almost everywhere among men and women, and has been promoted by several well-known Christian leaders. Men are excited about what they have read and are testifying that this is the answer they have been seeking.

However, a not-so-careful probe reveals the book to be a refried psychological model of masculinity taken from the secular mythopoetic (defined on page 18) men's movement of the 1980s and 1990s. And the worldview is anything but Christian; it is therapeutic to the bone (see Appendix 1). Of course this is not a strange discovery considering that Eldredge has a background in theater, and received training in 'Christianized' psychology.[2] But what does it say about our prominent leaders? It says they have either not read the book, or they themselves have been swallowed up by the therapeutic gospel. I tend to believe it is probably the latter.[3]

The psychological seduction of Christianity is the most subtle and widespread leaven in the church today. This leaven, which is changing the very constitution of orthodox Christian doctrine, consists of secular theories and techniques (there are over 1,500) nested in biblical concepts. Still, the basic assumptions of psychology, whether nested in Christian thought or not, are for the most part humanistic and non-biblical.

I am not saying psychology is of no use, I am only saying because of its nature, it must be kept in its proper place as a tool. It cannot be allowed (as is currently happening) to infringe on, and reshape the sound teachings of Scripture. If so, as we see in *Wild at Heart*, the result is a skewed view of the nature of man, sin, and God. In this we must remember the admonition of the apostle Paul to the Colossians:

> "See to it that no one takes you captive through philosophy and empty deception, according to the tradition of men, according to the elementary principles of the world, rather than according to Christ." (Colossians 2:8)

Wild at Heart is a wedding of psychology and Christian ideas. The message within its pages is biblically unsound and dangerous. Opening the pages of this book, I thought the goal was to learn about biblical masculinity, yet what I discovered was a self-focused *psycho-spiritual*[4] view of masculinity with Bible verses sprinkled on top. A message that was earthy to its core, which of course some might find commendable. I believe the message is destined to fall short and will leave men disappointed because of its terribly misguided orientation toward a man-centered gospel.

1

UNCOVERING THE SOURCE

Readers seem to think Eldredge got his revelations from the Bible because he is a Christian and quotes Bible verses. He tells us plainly though that he has received them from talking with "many, many men, reading literature, and gazing into boyhood dreams" (Eldredge 9). But there is more to the truth. The principles of the book are far from original with Eldredge, other than how he has tried to Christianize them.

Wild at Heart is not a new biblical teaching coming to the aid of crippled male virility, and neither is it an astute observation of human nature from a biblical grid. It is a retooled psychological model of masculinity taken primarily from the mythopoetic men's movement of the early 1990s. One of Eldredge's key links to this movement, as demonstrated by his use of content and quotes, is the grandfather of the mythopoetic movement, the writer/poet Robert Bly. It was his book, *Iron John*, that rang the masculine bell topping the best-seller list for much of 1991. Eldredge has capitalized on the elements of Bly's proven winner to do the same. To understand then, the guiding thought of *Wild at Heart*, one needs to first understand the mythopoetic men's movement and Bly (see Appendix 2, "A History of Bly").

Mythopoetic Men's Movement

This movement, from the 1980s and early 1990's, was called mythopoetic because of its reliance on mythical (legendary) archetypes (universal traits) for self-understanding. As men are connected through mythical stories to the universal qualities that characterize masculinity—the Hero, the Warrior, the King, the Wild Man, to name just a few—they touch elements of their masculine nature and are said to find healing.

The spiritual perspective of the mythopoetic men's movement is largely indebted to the ideas of psycho-theorist Carl Jung. The movement's adherents agree with Jung that men start life as whole persons but, through wounding (the *father wound*), lose their unity and become fragmented (Eldredge 75). The fallout from this father wound being a host of male social ills—a crisis in male identity, drug abuse, divorce, dysfunctional families, absent fathers, violent crime, and juvenile delinquency.

Eventually though, if men probe the archetypes (universal traits) buried in their subconscious, they will be able to heal these wounds and restore themselves to a state of wholeness and psycho-spiritual health. Consequently the whole mythopoetic men's movement is primarily a therapeutic effort at recovering wounded masculinity caused by fathers and the stresses of modernity (modern times). The thought is, if men return to what men always have been—wild, rough, and fierce—then they will find masculine health.

This is exactly what Eldredge is promoting but within a pseudo-biblical framework. Using secular movies, lyrics, poetry, cultural quotes, and Bible as the content of myth and story, he seeks to draw men into these '"universal masculine traits," which he claims are deeply spiritual. The dominating archetypes of his emphasis, which makes the thesis of his book, are what he calls the desire for adventure, battle, and a beauty to win. And he works early in the book to establish these as having their origins in the image of God in man, an attempt to validate and spiritualize their use.

> "There are three desires I find written so deeply into my heart I know now I can no longer disregard them without losing my soul. They are core to who and what I am and yearn to be. I gaze into boyhood, I search the pages of literature, I listen carefully to many, many men, and I am convinced these desires are universal, a clue into masculinity itself . . . in the heart of every man is a desperate desire for a battle to fight, an adventure to live, and a beauty to rescue. I want you to think of the films men love, the things they do with their free time, and especially the aspirations of little boys and see if I am not right on this" (Eldredge 9).

The Themes of *Wild at Heart*

In essence, all of the themes of the mythopoetic men's movement and Bly weave through Eldredge's *Wild at Heart*; the soft male/nice guy (Eldredge xi), lack of male identity (Eldredge Chapter 2), the father wound (60), masculine energy (55, 149), rituals of manhood (66), personal growth through spiritual discovery of the archetypes, and descending into one's spirit (125, 126).

Though there is some truth to these traits among men, they are not biblical paths to the integration and wholeness that is being sought, at least not from a Christian perspective. Eldredge cannot *sanitize* the mythopoetic and Bly with smatterings of Bible verses, and neither can he convert them into a biblical model of masculinity. They are what they are— the observations of a world looking for what it knows not.

Other Sources of Eldredge-*ology*

How does Eldredge get his universal insights into the nature of man? Besides Bly and others, he claims they come from his own recollection of boy hood, the literature he has read, and the "many, many men" he has talked with (Eldredge 9). He also says, "think of the films men love, the things they do with their free time, and especially the aspirations of boys and see if I am not right on this" (9). It is curious though, that he does not mention the Bible as a source for his understanding, unless of course it was included in the literature he had read. And it is equally as telling that the Bible has nothing to say about what Eldredge is proclaiming to be so universal among men. I am afraid our writer has substituted his own "-ology" for sound doctrine.

Why are movies important in *Wild at Heart*? As I have said, it is part of the indoctrination process. It is the method of the mythopoetic approach. Eldredge uses movies and stories to touch men in their emotions—in their masculine nature. In so doing he reinforces the thought that what he is saying is absolutely true. Again, as the song goes, "If it feels so right, how can it be so wrong?" After all, it is implied that these deep feelings that surface in response to manly movies are the true spirituality of a man, and when released, will set men free (Eldredge 9).

2

WILD AT HEART
A THERAPEUTIC GOSPEL

The affects of 21ˢᵗ century modern life have resulted in a diminishing capacity for truth. People no longer think in terms of right and wrong but in how they feel. Living what once was outward has been privatized and internalized into the regions of the *elusive heart*. The center of life has shifted. The world that was once moral is now therapeutic in nature. It is all about recovery, healing, feelings, and self-realization.

Think of the television commercials you have seen with therapeutic twists. Toyota, the company with the slogan "Get the Feeling," has a recent advertising campaign with a man declaring:

> "I used to start each day feeling inadequate, and powerless. But I didn't know why. My days were filled with anxiety and discomfort. No matter how hard I tried achieving my goals and aspirations, they seemed impossible. Then one day I met Dave. Dave

would introduce me to something that would change my life. The all new 2005 Toyota Tacoma. Now thanks to Tacoma, I am living my dream."

In a Yoplait yogurt commercial, four ladies are sitting around talking about how good the yogurt is, "Ooo, this is . . . day-at-the-spa-good." "No, this is . . . foot-massage good."

The jewelry commercial by Kay Jewelers announces, "Every kiss begins with Kay."

The slogan of Cingular is "The wireless company that believes in the value of self-expression."

And finally, in a commercial for Jeep, an artist instructing her students, "Today, we're doing self-portraits. But I want you to paint your soul!" The commercial ends with one of the students painting a Jeep.

All of these are representative of the therapeutic mindset that permeates our culture.

And the church has not escaped the cultural influences of the therapeutic. It too has become self-focused and reduced to preferences, feelings, and the pursuit of personal well-being. A scan of book titles in the local bookstore confirms the fact. The therapeutic self-help movement has become an entire publishing classification called "Christian psychology," tailored to help you find and repair yourself in the framework of spiritual growth. Titles include, *From Bondage to Bonding: Escaping Codependency, Embracing Biblical Love*, and *If I'm Forgiven, Why Do I Feel So Guilty?* The underlying premise of many of these books being, "I just want to be happy."

As the church becomes programmed with this kind of, "If it feels good it must be right" thinking, it looses its ability to discern and discriminate. As a result Christians choose churches and teaching on the bases of feelings rather than objective biblical facts. "If it feels true to me, it must be true." The results are devastating. *Wild at Heart* embodies this kind of teaching. It is a therapeutic gospel whose center is inward on self: its passions, healing, and recovery. It speaks very little of what is objective pertaining to living the Word of God, but a lot about what is psychological. Its message is clearly the secular philosophy of Bly and the mythopoetic movement. The results are predictable: people who have a moral framework built on answering the question, "How does it feel?"

The Therapeutic Gospel is Allergic to *What* is Moral

The therapeutic by its nature must take precedence over anything that might encroach upon personal and private feelings. This is because it depends on the liberty of personal preference. So its need for self-expression to survive makes it allergic to the transcendent and objective quality of morality with its demand for accountability.

Morality by its nature calls for conformity that transcends the personal and private and is binding on all. Because Eldredge is writing from a therapeutic worldview, he by necessity must place the heart and its feelings over what is moral. Early in the book Eldredge established this point. From the opening introduction he says, men need "permission to live from the heart and not from the list of 'shoulds' and 'ought tos'" (Eldredge xi). The recovery of the masculine heart is first the recovery of a heart free "from the list of 'should' and 'ought to' that has left so many [men] tired and bored." He says men need permission to loose themselves from the stereotype of what "a good husband / father / Christian / churchgoer" ought to be (xi).

At first glance this seems to make sense. It sounds like he is just trying to help men come out from under the dead works of the law into a life of freedom. We all know how some in Christianity want to saddle us with rules and regulations.

But this is not the case. Eldredge is not addressing the problem of work's righteousness; he is striving to alleviate the tension that is created by moral demand in a therapeutic world. In reality the moral dimensions of the gospel, which transcend one's own personal persuasions with objective demands, are a hindrance to Eldredge's therapeutic worldview.

What does the church do, Eldredge asks? He says it has "done some terrible things to men" in an effort to raise a standard of '"dutifulness" as a mark of Christian maturity (Eldredge 7). He suggests that men learn to live the higher life, but his idea of the higher spirituality is not what it appears to be. It is a marginalizing of morals in favor of men living from their hearts—living according to their own personal preferences and deep masculine passions. This cavalier attitude toward morality is troublesome and destructive to a Christ-centered and biblical worldview.

Instead of asking, "What must I do to be a better person?" the question according to Eldredge should be, "What makes you come alive?" (Eldredge 9). This again is the therapeutic worldview mitigating against a biblical moral view. It is feeling and passion over moral virtues lived from a life in Christ. Shouldn't the answer to, "What makes you come alive?" be, "being filled with the Holy Spirit?" (Ephesians 5:18). That message is nowhere to be found in *Wild at Heart.*

Christianity is most certainly about freedom and not legalism, but it is not without the fabric of the moral nature of God. You can live morally without the life of Christ, but you cannot live the life of Christ without morality. The Scripture says, "Let him who names the name of Christ depart from iniquity" (2 Timothy 2:19). Eldredge's is too reckless toward the moral nature of Christianity.

The Life of Christ is Passionately Moral

Eldredge has identified men living in duty without life, and he has rightly said they are tired and bored. His answer to this condition is a rediscovering of masculine passions that he believes will put zest back into men's lives. However, nothing could be further from the truth. These masculine passions are not the same as the life of Christ.

The problem is not that men are stuck in external morality with no heart as Eldredge suggests. The real issue is that men have not been significantly filled with the life of Christ. They have not been filled with the Spirit of God. When that happens, men will not need to be instructed in passion, and surely not in masculine passion. They will, by the indwelling Spirit, be passionate for God and for living in righteousness. And there will be no careless attitude toward morality. They will desire to do what is right and to fulfill moral duty from the heart. That is the nature of the Holy Spirit when He comes to live within us.

The true life of Christ is passionately moral, not because of a rediscovered manliness, but because of the person of Christ within. Eldredge's message is confusing in regards to what motivates and empowers true godly living. He is mistaken in thinking that natural masculinity is somehow the true foundation of godly passion. It is a disservice to men and the church to put moral duty in a second-class category, while raising in its place a supposedly liberated heart free in its masculine passions.

God is not a Therapist

Theologian David Wells comments that, somehow we have come to "imagine that the great purposes of life are psychological rather than moral." However, God is not a therapist and the gospel is not a promise of personal well-being, free of all personal pains and conflicts.[5] Salvation is not primarily about a journey of inner healing nor the restoring of some mythological masculinity, it is about righteousness—imputed and lived. God is holy and he is calling men to live before him in passionate moral purity by the power of the Holy Spirit. It seems that Eldredge prefers to live in a therapeutic world of elusive feelings rather than the moral world of "accountable" righteousness.

When the apostle Paul speaks of grace he says nothing about finding one's lost heart, living by masculine passion, or healing the father wound, but he says everything about doing what is right. He says that grace leads us to deny what is immoral. Consider his words:

> "For the grace of God that bringeth salvation hath appeared to all men, Teaching us that, denying ungodliness and worldly lusts, we should live soberly, righteously, and godly, in this present world." (Titus 2:11,12)

It is without a doubt that masculinity should find its greatest expression not in a rediscovering of manly passions, but by being filled with the instruction of biblical grace. Again, the message of *Wild at Heart* has done us a disservice. It has erroneously taught that masculine passion constitutes the essence of Christian manhood instead of biblical grace.

Therapeutic Language—a Clue

Even biblical language has been reshaped under the influence of the therapeutic worldview. The words of sound doctrine have been substituted with psycho-therapeutic language, which is typically devoid of clear biblical meaning. *Wild at Heart* has this sickness. Though it may sound biblical, it is pseudo-spiritual.

Wild at Heart: A Therapeutic Gospel

The therapeutic phrases like "deep masculinity," "father wound," "strength gone bad," "deep heart," "the true you," and "'grieving your wound," are not representative of clear biblical content but instead give us a clue as to their therapeutic nature. They are expressions of the subjective, which are wholly relative to the hearer. They are not representations of what is moral, absolute, and accountable. A person with a Christian background may or may not think of the phrase "grieving your wound" as a statement of repentance. It could just as easily be thought of in terms of self-piety, as it seems to be in *Wild at Heart*. The point is, these therapeutic terms are hard to pin down and not representative of clear biblical doctrine. In contrast, when the Bible says to "repent" of your "sin," this is a clear representation of biblical meaning with no hint of elusiveness.

An example of what I am speaking about is Eldredge's view of a man's addictions. Instead of affirming them as sin, he substitutes a new idea, "A man's addictions are the result of his refusing his strength" (Eldredge 149). In doing this the moral responsibility is diminished, what is sin is now redefined as a therapeutic concept—refusing strength. Essential biblical thought is crowded out and replaced with what is error, secondary, and not vital.

The following is a letter I received from a young man expressing how Eldredge has helped him:

> "*Wild at Heart* really spoke to me deeply because I was raised without a father and when he came around he was usually drunk and abusive . . . [it] has helped me understand some of the patterns that my life has taken and it has encouraged me to draw closer to Jesus to find the healing of my hurts."

I would in no way discount what the Lord may have done in this young man's life or in any others for that matter. Surely Jesus heals inward hurts and redirects the sinful patterns of our lives and for that I rejoice. I am grateful for any way the Lord might have worked through some portion of this book for the betterment of a hurting soul. Nevertheless, my continued concern is that the content of this letter is representative of a therapeutic orientation and not a biblical one, which I believe is a peek into the emerging mindset of 21st century Christianity.

3

THE HEART IS NOT THE CENTRAL THEME OF THE BIBLE

Eldredge replaces what is central to Christianity with a new center. He places the heart at the center of Christian faith, "The heart is the central theme in Scripture and the most important part of any person—including God."[6] The heart is an important theme, but it is secondary at best. The central thesis of the Bible is Christ and the cross. What Eldredge has done is to create a man-centered gospel. This is in accordance with the nature of a therapeutic gospel.

Eldredge talks of surrender to Christ, "We yield our lives to the One who is our life" (Eldredge 128), and he sounds very orthodox. But then in the same context he begins to turn the gospel inward by saying we are to invite Jesus into the "broken and unhealed places of our heart." And he adds, "When the Bible tells us that Christ came to "redeem mankind" it offers a whole lot more than forgiveness" (128). He says the core of Christ's mission was to heal, "restore and release you, your soul, the true you [what is the true you?]" (129).

29

Though the Lord is certainly concerned about healing our lives, Eldredge's statement is once again the work of a therapeutic mindset resetting the center of Christianity manward. It is marginalizing the moral dimensions (*forgiveness* is a moral term), which have to do with our sin and relationship with God—his holiness and character—and replacing them with a focus on man's need of inner healing. In doing this Eldredge is implying that recovery and inner healing are the primary concern, although they are not. Salvation is first about the cross and imputed righteousness. Only secondarily is it about healing the heart or restoring masculinity.

Psychological Theories or the Word of God?

Wild at Heart has this cultural disease of the therapeutic worldview and will ultimately leave its readers hollow. Though the book appears wise and promises that when the true heart is rediscovered, boredom, unhappiness, lack of meaning, lack of freedom, and failed relationships will be satisfied, it cannot deliver. How can it do so when it contains no biblical foundation? Of course, there are Scriptures in the book, but they are more like Hamburger Helper (an additive that makes a meal go further) than sound doctrine.[7] In fact, Eldredge's supposed search for the heart, with its sprinklings of religious and secular rhetoric, has little to do with the Word of God. It has a lot to do with nothing, other than to give a prescription of a borrowed secular masculinity that can only produce the sorrow of self-absorption in the name of Christ.

The kind of life that Eldredge prescribes (and I am not sure he knows what that is, because he says he is still looking for his own heart (Eldredge 3)) will never be found through the techniques of self-disclosure or healing of the wounded soul. Neither will it be found in men becoming more aggressive, adventurous, passionate, or gazing into their boyhood dreams. The only real answers for godly masculinity are to be found in the pages of the Bible, however that is not where Eldredge directs his readers. For him, spending many hours with his friend and partner fly-fishing, backpacking, and hanging out in pubs (bars) is where he says he has found healing (128). And when he needs to hear from God he finds his answers in the movies, "Why does something in my heart feel orphaned? The answer came [to him] through several movies."

Aren't the Scriptures Sufficient?

Now God can speak through a movie or a donkey for that matter, but why doesn't Eldredge turn men to the Scripture and prayer instead of backpacking and movies? I think the answer is obvious; he has not valued Scripture. So it is not surprising when he informs us that the deep desires of the heart, are themselves telling us the truth about the life we were meant to live (Eldredge 18).

Eldredge would be well-advised to steer his readers out of themselves and their deep wounds to embracing the written Word of God with the intent of living it. Neither our deepest desires, nor a new masculinity filled with passion and adventure, will ever provide the transforming power men so desperately need. No light can be found by men looking inward into their own hearts and desires. Only the Word of God is a lamp unto our feet and a light unto our path. Only it can give true salvation and transform us into the likeness of Christ, who alone is the greatest model of masculinity.

The path to maturity as a man of God is simply living the Scripture. In other words, the Scripture is sufficient!

> "All scripture [is] given by inspiration of God, and [is] profitable for doctrine, for reproof, for correction,

31

for instruction in righteousness: That the man of God may be perfect (mature), thoroughly furnished unto all good works." (2 Timothy 3:16-17)

4

Making God Into the Image of Man

A major premise of Eldredge's theology of male masculinity is that the traits of masculinity—its nature, desires, needs, and passions—are equated to truth itself. This is because he believes they are given by God and therefore must be of God (Eldredge 18).

Because we are made in the image of the Lord, then what we are naturally is what God is. Thus, from the image of God in man spring desires that speak the truths about who and what man is. Truths that man only need to discover to be free. Eldredge asks, "What if those deep desires in our hearts are telling us the truth, revealing to us the life we were meant to live?" (Eldredge 18).

But this is more than a "what if" with Eldredge. Listen to his words: "Adventure is a deeply spiritual longing written into the soul of man" (Eldredge 5), and there "are three desires I find written so deeply into my heart I know now I can no longer disregard them without losing my soul" (9).[7] He clearly equates the desires of the masculine heart with spiritual truth. This is a dangerous flaw in his thinking. And so the erroneous thought: to recover these deep masculine traits is to recover truth that will restore manhood and wholeness. This idea is the beginning of a confusion that permeates the entire book.

Is Masculinity a Trait of God?

Eldredge seems to have misconceived what it means to be made in the image of God. He seems to think it's about human masculine and feminine traits. It is not. The thought that men and women bear the image of God as gender is not a biblical concept. This thought also doesn't take into account the fallen condition of man.

Man in his natural state is distorted and is not what God is. Those deep desires that Eldredge says might be telling the truth (Eldredge 5) are coming from a corrupted nature. For this reason, a biblical model of male masculinity cannot be built from the inclinations of the heart. When Eldredge proclaims masculine passions as spiritual and good, and "every man is a stem of that victorious stock," he is clouding the doctrine of the depravity of man (27, 35).[8] Men cannot be left to think that there is something good in them. They must say with Paul the apostle, "Within me dwells no good thing" (Romans 7:18). In Christ every man is a stem, and Christ is the treasure within, but Eldredge does not make that clear.

Eldredge desires to bring back what he sees as the true image of God since men are to bear that image. He tells us, "God's design—which he [God] places in boys as a picture of himself—is a resounding yes" to be fierce, wild, and passionate (Eldredge 31). God is a warhorse and a stallion though the church has basically turned Him into an old lady. The conclusion is, because God is really a warhorse, so are men: "The boy is a warrior" and, "Every man is a stem of that victorious stock" (27). Quoting Isaiah 63:1-4, he tells us that this *Braveheart* kind of God is, "One fierce, wild, and passionate guy." And now He is, "Cheerfully and heroically living in dynamic relationship with His fallen world and loves to 'come through' for it. God loves to show us like the good male role model He is, and that He has what it takes" (31).

Our Base Nature Doesn't Reveal God

What Eldredge is doing is trying to rescue us from what he believes to be our mistaken image of God, and especially of Jesus, that he is weak and old-lady-like. He is trying to draw a caricature of God that lifts God up and out of the likes of a Mother Teresa, and sets him on high with the *Braveheart* type of William Wallace (Eldredge 22). Yet, once again, Eldredge is casting God into the image of man: a wild and passionate guy, a *Braveheart* loving to come through, a good male role model showing us he has what it takes.

According to Eldredge, God made Adam in his image—fierce, wild, and passionate, and then Eve, God's finishing touch. Then Adam said, "Wow!" Eldredge also says God is the strength revealed in man and the seductive beauty revealed in woman (Eldredge 37). This may all sound biblical, but it isn't. Eldredge is looking to the base nature of humanity to discover who God is. Only the special revelation of the word of God can do that. This is the influence of the therapeutic always trying to make God conformable to its own image.

It is true, man is a warrior and God is described in Scripture as a warrior, but this is not who God is, and this doesn't sanctify this human character trait as spiritual. Eldredge has misunderstood the use of biblical language and ascribed to God the image of man. He has thought God to be like us. But this is absurdity. This is anthropomorphizing God (making God in the image of man). Though the Bible is filled with anthropomorphic expressions (God is a warrior, God is jealous), it is erroneous to draw the conclusion that these traits are godly. This confusion is cleared though, when one understands that the transcendent (beyond) God has used biblical language as a means of conveying truth through the medium of human ideas and thoughts.

The image of God in man rests in man's moral bent, conscience, and purpose. A standard reformed (reformation theology) way of understanding what it means to be made in God's image is that God's image is not found in a particular aspect of humanness, but is first understood in terms of the human task, office, and calling. According to the church Father Thomas Aquinas, it is the intellectual soul, which makes the human person to be in the image of God. This is neither caused by the male, nor is it essentially different in man and woman.[9]

If true manhood is the goal, then Christ is the only answer and he never called us to live by rediscovering or renewing our gender nature. But he did call us to be born again and to live by moral duty and character—to be the servant of all, to be meek and humble, to consider others better than ourselves, to lay our lives down, to express our love of Christ through obedience to his commandments.

What Makes Men Great?

Eldredge wants to save men by bringing them back to what he believes once made men great, to what he claims is the real heart-beat of the true masculine identity—a longing for adventure, battle, and a beauty to win (Eldredge xi). This is how he says man bears the image of God. But what makes men great is not defined by human traits of masculinity.

Men by natural inclination do love adventure, battles, and beauties, but these natural elements are not the stuff of greatness. In contrast, the Bible says that greatness will be in the one who is the servant of all. The Bible defines greatness in terms of humility and servant-hood. It is confusing to equate characteristics of creature-hood with biblical truth about man and God.

Romanticizing God

We are also told God has a romantic heart as well as a fierce one. A woman is more seductive than fierce, and Eve and her daughters are also a stem of the victorious stock (Eldredge 37). Like the design of a man [boy], Eldredge believes the seductive beauty of the woman is also trying to tell us something of God. God desires to know, as does every woman, "Why won't you choose me?" God wants to be loved: He wants to be someone's priority (36). And how does Eldredge know this? "Why else would God have made woman as He did? Why would He have made things like wine, music, and poetry and created places like Hawaii and the Bahamas? Whose idea was it to make a kiss so delicious?" (33). And the tragedy he tells us is not only has the church missed this, but theologians have missed this truth as well (32). However, this romanticizing of God is just another means of remaking God into the image of man.

Uncovering Wild at Heart

5

SEARCH FOR THE LOST HEART

Eldredge tells us that he is "simply searching, as many men are, for an authentic masculinity," and that he is "looking for his heart" (Eldredge 13). Still, the whole search is nowhere commended in Scripture. If there were something to be recovered, then it would be implied that something good was in man all along. Thus the doctrine of original sin could not stand.

This whole idea of recovery really comes from Bly and the world of psychology. Psychology—even Christianized brands—lean toward the thought that buried within every human is an inherent good that is just waiting be discovered and released. But this generally only serves to subvert the biblical doctrine of sin. Rather than clearly stating the depravity of man, it digs deep to discover some good thing that is buried, usually due to hurt. This is what I believe Eldredge is implying.

In tune with Bly, Eldredge wants to bring men back to what he envisions as the true model of male masculinity. He wants them to rediscover their masculine hearts, which are wild and free.

He starts this anthropology by picturing Adam as being born a wild man in the outback while Eve was born in the Garden of Eden (Eldredge 3). This he says is one of the reasons men are so longing to return to the wild.

Eldredge asks, and what has happened to men? "They have lost their hearts due to modernity [modern life]." They have been driven into "remote regions of the soul" (whatever that means). He says though modernity has domesticated their hearts, "The core of a man's heart is undomesticated and that is good" (Eldredge 4). It is only as man returns to his undomesticated [wild] self that he will be able to answer the deep fundamental questions of his male nature: Who am I? What am I made of? What am I destined for? (5).

We are also told that these answers are not found in domesticated settings, but "out there on the burning desert sands" (Eldredge 6). However, it would seem to me that the answers to these questions would be in the Bible, not in the burning desert sands.

He continues saying men are made for the "rhythms of the earth" and the "roughness of rope". They are made for what boys dreamed of (what biblical category is that?) (Eldredge 6), but society has belittled and softened men.

Eldredge doesn't just blame society, he also blames the church for having done terrible things to men (7). He says the church has turned men into good boys rewarding them for doing their duty while they die in their hearts. Like the fathers who have wounded their children, so he says the church has caused men's hearts to die.

The Power to Set Men Free

Now I believe Eldredge wants to present a life of freedom over one of dead religion. He has a vision of men being free to live passionately with meaning as opposed to being caged in rules and regulations. However, the power to loose men out of dead religion and stereotypes is not found in healing the father wound or in blaming the church for raising a standard. And neither is it found in slipping into a new suit of manly passions. As I have said previously, it is discovered in having and living a life in Christ, which includes moral responsibility.

The Scripture says that some have a form of godliness but deny the power thereof. It appears Eldredge has observed men in whom this is true. They are men who live bland dutiful lives but who have no power. And so, his solution is a return to raw masculinity, yet this is not a recovery of the power but a further denying of it. The power of a godly life is in having a heart filled with God. A dynamic Spirit-filled life is not going to be caged. It's impossible. And when the heart is alive because of Christ, moral duty will not be a burden but a joy, "For this is the love of God, that we keep His commandments. And His commandments are not burdensome" (1 John 5:3).

Why are Men Bored?

Eldredge infers that tired and bored men are Christians, but are they really? And if people are inwardly dead, is it because they have lost their hearts of manliness through being domesticated? Or is it because they have lost, or never really had, a life in Christ? So what Eldredge is proposing as the dynamism of godly men can never answer the problem. His is still a Christianity that has a form of godliness but denies the power thereof. The following is a letter I received from a young man that makes the point:

"I've been reading *Wild at Heart* (it was pushed heavily at a recent men's conference our church sponsored), and I've been enjoying it because I too am convinced that men have suffered by allowing themselves to be feminized and disconnected from nature and some of our natural urges to hunt, explore, and otherwise live out some degree of wildness. Yet there were substantial parts of the book that just did not ring true.

Your review is by far the most cogent discussion of the flaws in Eldredge's thinking. And maybe that is what has been eating at me—the idea that so much of the book is just "what I think" vs. what Scripture would lead a thinking person to believe. In the end, I am persuaded by your observation that perhaps I am not a tired and bored Christian, but rather a tired and bored man who has not really truly and deeply accepted Christ. If only our pastors, family and friends would be so straightforward what a different world this might be.

Thank you. I appreciate your willingness to produce and publish such a thoughtful and objective piece."

Once more, only a heart filled with the power of a yielded life to Christ, His Spirit and Word, will make true godly men and women. Deep gender passion is no substitute for the power of the indestructible life.

Men Know It But They Can't Explain It

Eldredge continues to blame the church for the condition of men by saying the problem with the church is that it has not invited men to know and live from their deep hearts (Eldredge

8). The heart, he says, is missing from men because it has been misunderstood, and through abuse, driven as a wounded animal into the high country of the soul. Women know it, and men know it though they can't explain it. The hearts of men are on the run. With this said, Eldredge makes the claim that God wants to invite men to live out of their masculine hearts. So for a person to really find himself, he must rediscover his masculine (feminine) heart—which is what God created and placed in him.

Many want what Eldredge is talking about, but the solution, as I have been saying, is not in some recovery of natural masculinity, it is in the passion of a Spirit-filled and empowered life in Christ. Then the duty of virtue will be life and blessing, and not death (see Appendix 3, "What is Grace?").

I pose this question: Is the biblical view of masculinity an invitation for men to live out of their true masculine hearts? Or is it a command to live out of Christ? I don't know of any invitations, but I do know a command: "But now (God) commands all men everywhere to repent" (Acts 17:30). The only real model of manhood is to put on the Lord Jesus Christ and to make no provision for the flesh.

Scandalous Valiant Women

Like the model of masculinity, Eldredge's model of femininity has three essential components: a woman yearns to be fought for, an adventure to share, and to be the beauty unveiled. This is why she plays dress-up her whole life. "Do you see me?" asks the heart of every girl (Eldredge 17). And Eldredge says, "Christianity has missed her heart as well." He says the only thing offered the feminine soul by the church is pressure to be a good servant. There is no one to fight for her, no one to sweep her up into adventure and she rightly wonders

43

if she has any beauty to unveil (17).

No doubt about it Eldredge says, Christian woman are . . . "tired." Eldredge promotes that the true design of a woman is to be "valiant, vulnerable, and scandalous" (Eldredge 190), which he says is a far cry from "church ladies." Again, these traits, as real as they may be, do not represent a biblical model of femininity. I would rather have a church full of tired servants than scandalous valiant women because servant-hood is a biblical virtue. Being scandalous is not.

Eldredge says the feminine soul is pressured to be a good servant as if that is a form of abuse. Yet this is the very thing that the Bible calls her (all of us) to be. The Bible says women are, "to be discreet, chaste, homemakers, good, obedient to their own husbands, that the word of God may not be blasphemed" (Titus 2:5). The Bible says nothing about a woman being valiant, vulnerable, or seductive.

Paul also says that women are to, "adorn themselves . . . with good works" (1 Timothy 2:9,10). He says that this is becoming of women who profess godliness. Where is this view of femininity in *Wild at Heart*? It is not there because Eldredge has to dip into the wells of secular psychology to find his model of femininity as he did for masculinity.

The Madness Continues

And so the madness continues, with Eldredge contrasting the image of a man as a nice guy with that of a dangerous guy, and a woman as a tired servant with that of one who is captivating and seductive. "Which would you rather have said of you— that you are a tired worker, or that you are a captivating woman?" With that Eldredge rests his case. He says the answers are obvious (Eldredge 18). What is obvious is that this is a non-biblical view of both masculinity and femininity.

44

6

SIN OR VICTIMIZATION?

Eldredge tells us it's no coincidence that many men fall into an affair not for love, not even for sex, but by their own admission, for adventure. This is because men have been told to put away adventure and to live only for duty (Eldredge 43). Eldredge goes on to say that if a man does not find those things for which his heart is made, and if he is not invited to live from his deep heart, he will look for it in some other way—pornography, affairs, and lustful living.

According to Eldredge, because a man has been defrauded of his real heart, he longs for "the beauty" but doesn't know how to relate to her. He is drawn to her but it is all a mystery to him. So, victimized and confused by his loss of heart, a man turns secretly to the imitation—pornography. And this is extremely addictive to him because it makes him feel like a man. He says this is because the less a man feels like a real man in the presence of a real woman: the more vulnerable he is to pornography (Eldredge 44). And so, man's heart denied the very things it most deeply desires, is driven into dark regions and, "every man knows that something has gone wrong . . . they just don't know what it is" (44).

Now what is it that Eldredge is saying here? He is not telling us men are sinners. He is not telling us men are guilty. Instead, he is telling us men have been victimized and it is not their fault. Because men have not been invited to live from their "deep hearts" but told to be good, they have lost their way falling into affairs and addictions like pornography.

It's Not My Fault

Eldredge says men are just confused, they know something is wrong but can't get a handle on what it is. He implies that if men only knew how, they would live right. He says they have been defrauded by having to suppress who they really are, and what they most deeply need.

They get around a woman and don't feel like a real man, so they become vulnerable to pornography. And it's not their fault. Then I ask, whose fault is it? Even if what Eldredge is saying is true, who is to blame? No one is to blame but the man himself. He is responsible for his own life. He alone is the sinner by his own choice.

This is what the therapeutic gospel does. It makes a man's failures and lusts anything but sin, and allows men to shift the blame to something or someone else. In so doing the biblical concept of sin is gutted. The man does not have to take responsibility for his sin because he has an excuse. It is not his fault. He is the victim.

The message of *Wild at Heart* is guilty of shifting the responsibility and guilt of sin away from men, producing in them a victim mentality. In this it is discounting the true meaning of sin.

Was the Sin of Adam Only a Weakness?

According to Eldredge, God does not warn Adam of the impending danger coming in the temptation of his wife Eve. He comments that this is because God believed in Adam—that he would do what he was designed to do—"Come through in a pinch" (Eldredge 50). He then tells us that Adam failed Eve and humanity because he would not risk, and fight, and rescue Eve in the moment of trial. Adam denied his masculine nature and went passive, and is a case of masculine strength gone bad. And now, every man repeats this sin of Adam (51). He allows his strength to go bad. But the problem is not strength gone bad. What Eldredge has done is misrepresent the nature of sin. He has redefined it as a weakness rather than what it really is, rebellion against a holy God.

Not only is this a misrepresentation of the fall of man, it is an erroneous interpretation of what the Bible is saying. Eldredge's commentary is pure imagination. It's what we call in theology *isogesis*—reading one's own opinion into the Bible text. Eldredge is reading his therapeutic premises into the biblical story of the creation of man.

One thing is sure about the text in Genesis, it doesn't say Adam lost his nerve and failed to exercise his manhood in protecting Eve. He sinned through disobedience to God's commandment, and in so doing plunged the whole moral universe into decay and death. It was not a failure of passive manhood on Adam's part; it was a failure of moral proportions. Adam did not have a lapse of masculine weakness, but he denied God—he sinned! And why is it that Eldredge interprets these verses as man failing humanity, rather than man failing God? That is because his message is a therapeutic / man-centered gospel.

Is Sin Masculine Strength Gone Bad?

A therapeutic model of reality shies away from the concept of sin or at least tames it by calling it another name. From Eldredge's position, sin is not about moral disobedience to a holy God, it is about repressed passion and masculinity. It is about "masculine strength gone bad."

This is what we see when Eldredge mentions the murder of Abel by Cain. He doesn't call the murder of Abel, sin; he says it was "strength gone bad" (Eldredge 55). From Eldredge's point of view, Cain just ran from his strength and allowed it to become violent (see Bly's archetype of the Savage or Soft Man, Appendix 2). He failed to answer the question, "Am I really a man? Have I got what it takes . . . when it counts?" (57). If Cain had these questions answered, if he could have taken the advice of *Wild at Heart*, he possibly would not have committed his indiscretion (sin) of killing his brother Abel.

It appears, Eldredge doesn't believe sin is the problem, at least from God's view. He tells us that, "too many Christians believe their hearts are wicked." Not anymore he says, because "we have new hearts" (Jeremiah 31:33). "Sin is no longer the deepest thing about us. God only sees our new hearts and they are good" (Eldredge134). Once again Eldredge is simply diminishing the biblical view of sin in favor of a therapeutic one. The biblical view of sin is about disobedience to God and individual responsibility. The therapeutic view of sin is about misguided weakness, which is not man's fault.

The Origin of the Father Wound

The motif of the *father wound* is not only from Bly, but also from psychologist John Lee who was also involved in the early men's movements. In his book, *At My Father's Wedding*, he describes this idea of the father wound, which Eldredge has woven into his *Wild at Heart.*

Lee tells us that fathers have wounded their sons deeply by their abusive and/or passive natures, their unreasonable expectations, and their inability to hear their own sons' anger. He believes the father wound is universal to all men and that this wound is the source of all the negative issues of men—their addictions, failed relationships, inner conflicts, and low self-esteem.

Lee says there is hope for healing though. If these negative images (Eldredge calls them "messages" (Eldredge 72)) given by fathers can be "killed" off, then a new image of masculinity can be raised that will make men whole. They will rediscover a "deep masculinity." In blaming the father for the failings of men, Lee (as well as Eldredge) is saying that it is not their fault. Lee also encourages men to get into mentoring relationships with other men to clear away the isolationism, and to discover their "sword," "shield," and true masculinity (more masculine archetypes). A major part of the therapy directs men to get in touch with their past hurt and anger.

All of these themes are advanced in *Wild at Heart:* every man has been wounded by his father (Eldredge 60), most of a man's issues spring from that injury (72), the hope of true masculinity is in healing the father wound and rediscovering one's deep masculinity, and it is not the man's fault. As I have already said, these themes may read as truth because they describe common conditions with which men can identify. But make no mistake, they are not pathways to a biblical masculinity, they are more of a journey into the fallen nature of man.

Victimized Men

Eldredge says our churches are full of men who are examples of weak, sweet, courteous, mind-your-manners kind of people, men who have been wounded in their strength multiple times (Eldredge 82). (Again this is simply the anthropology of Bly, Lee, and others).

A man, he says, should be dangerous and heroic. Like a stallion, he is strong, "very strong" and has a mind of his own. They don't like to be bridled and are aggressive especially if mares are around. If you want a tamer animal, then *castrate* him. A gelding is much more compliant (Eldredge 84). But if you want the life of a stallion, you have to have an element of danger.

Eldredge compares the state of men's hearts to the tragedy of the men who stormed the beaches of Omaha in WWII. He says:

> "Look around and see the carnage. There is no passion for freedom, no fighting will, the women are not grateful for men who have loved them well. Men have been taken out and lie with shattered lives, dying in their souls due to the wounds they have received. They have lost heart. It is the Omaha Beach of the soul." (Eldredge 85)

I don't doubt the pain and sorrow in people's lives and the wounds men have encountered. It is true the church is full of syrupy feminized men, the kind who can't lead their families much less the church, and who default their responsibilities to others. I am sure these men can readily identify with the images of a gelding or of being on Omaha Beach. These are powerful word pictures that many men can relate to. But again, they do not represent the truth from a biblical perspective. Instead, what Eldredge has dramatically painted is a masculinity that blames others, and allows men to shun responsibility in their lives. It is not a picture of a true man in Christ.

God is furious about what has happened to men, according to Eldredge. He quotes Luke 17:2 as the expression of anger God has towards what has wounded them: "It would be better to be thrown into the sea with a large millstone tied around the neck than to face the punishment in store for harming one of these little ones."

Here Eldredge is identifying a man's pain and wound as injury inflicted on a "little one"—the man. He makes men feel sorry for themselves. God surely has pity on the plight of all people, but Eldredge is making the wounds of sin part of a victimization structure that men cannot help, and are not responsible for. He is transforming sin into a wound, and its guilt and responsibility into someone else's fault.

Our writer says it is because of this battle, and the fact that it has not been acknowledged that many men feel abandoned or betrayed by God (Eldredge 85). "No one ever told them they were being moved to the front lines . . ." (85). A man's wound is not his fault (125). It is this gelding of a man that has left him dying in his soul. But if you ever got your heart back, Eldredge comments, you would be dangerous big time. You would do a lot of damage on the side of good, because you and your heart are good—you are a stem of the victorious stalk (87).

But all this psycho-macho talk is totally ridiculous. It is just more of the same—victimization. Now the issue is, "No one ever told them." This is pitiful in my estimation. And then, "If you ever get your heart back you will do a lot of damage, because you and your heart are good." What is this saying? It is saying absolutely nothing from a biblical perspective. This is the gospel of humanism and it is man-centered to the core. Eldredge wants men to live from their core (Eldredge 75), yet the Bible wants men to live from Christ, then they will be truly dangerous. Consider these words of Paul:

"I am crucified with Christ: nevertheless I live; yet
not I, but Christ liveth in me: and the life which I
now live in the flesh I live by the faith of the Son of
God, who loved me, and gave himself for me."
(Galatians 2:20)

Why Do Men Get into Pornography?

Why is pornography the number one addiction?
Eldredge answers. It is the seductive beauty of a woman reaching
down into a man's desperate hungry soul that is longing for
validation. The quest of men for the *golden-haired woman* is
mythological in scope (another archetype) (Eldredge 91). It is a
quest for man's lost masculinity and to be the hero. The addiction
of pornography is a man's famished heart searching for the
validation of the golden haired woman.

Here, one more time, we are given additional excuses for
victimization. Once again it is not a man's fault, he gets into
pornography because he has not received proper validation. The
Bible does not make excuses for sin. It says it is a work of the flesh
and those who live that way will not enter into the Kingdom of
God. Sin is not a sickness that can be cured if one finds its cause.
Sin is rebellion against God and can only be dealt with by repentance
toward God and obedient faith towards Christ.

What Makes a Homosexual?

And what makes a man homosexual? Eldredge says it is a
heart hungry for masculine love. It is a result of men trying to
repair the "wound" with the masculine strength they feel they do
not possess (Eldredge 94, 95). Yet the Bible says, "And likewise also
the men, leaving the natural use of the woman, burned in their lust
one toward another" (Romans 1:26). This verse says nothing about

them being victimized but that "when they knew God, they glorified Him not as God" (Romans 1:21).

Eldredge does not claim either pornography or homosexuality to be sin, rather he says they are a deep hunger of the misplaced masculine soul that is trying to be satisfied. The implication is that it is not their fault and they are the victims of unmet needs. It is a tragedy that this kind of thinking would be projected as somehow Christian. It is a still greater tragedy that so many men and women would read this book and buy into this distortion of biblical truth.

Uncovering Wild at Heart

7

THE DOCTRINE OF THE FALSE SELF

Eldredge quotes author Brennan Manning, "Spiritual life begins with the acceptance of our wounded self" and then picks up on Manning's idea of the false self, neither of which are biblically true (Eldredge 106). On the contrary, spiritual life does not begin by accepting one's wounded self, but by accepting the guilt of one's sins against a Holy God. And there is hardly a biblical category for Manning's false self other than what the Bible calls the carnal man, which is real enough.

My False Self Did It

According to Eldredge, it is from the place of woundedness that men construct false selves as defense mechanisms to protect them from their own hurts and pains; the lies of the false self are shattered, then the true self can be healed and released (Eldredge 108). The false self is said to be the sin and the real problem, not you. "The real you is on the side of God against the false self" (145).

Eldredge further says the big lie in the church is to say that we are sinners. According to Ezekiel 36:26 all Christians have new hearts and are thus free from sin. It is our false self that does the sinning.

The solution then, is to "drop the fig leaf (false self); come out from hiding . . . let the wound surface from beneath it all" (Eldredge 112). Deal with the sinful false self we are told, and the buried pain will be healed allowing the sinless *true you* to emerge. But what is this dichotomy of self? Sin and its responsibility cannot be conveniently placed on some invented false self as if that is somehow not really you. There is only one you, and you are responsible before God for all your sins. When the Day of Judgment arrives, no one will be saying, "My false self made me do it." No, each will be accountable for their own sin before God.

Another question: Where does Eldredge teach responsibility towards God for sin? It is auspiciously missing. Like good therapeutic theology, *Wild at Heart* is not about repenting; it is about getting in touch with wounds and being healed. This false self theology, which is an invention of Manning, is nothing more than a design to give people an excuse for not taking personal responsibility for their sins. It is a sleight of hand, "I am not responsible for sin, my false self did it, and I am on the side of God against the false self." This is not the gospel of the Bible.

And so Manning, and now Eldredge, invite us to be free from posing (lying) and to live in our true selves. Then (according to Manning and Eldredge) we will be all we were meant to be. We will be authentic with no games or masks. "You're not the problem, it is your poser self," we are told. And Eldredge makes this all sound so urgent and vital. We are told this is the great quest for which God is fiercely committed.

Maybe I am just old-fashioned and out of touch, but where is mention of the blood of Christ, or the holiness and justice of God? Where is sin? What is the definition of sin? It is surely not what the will know Bible teacher R.C. Sproul describes as, "cosmic treason to the King of Kings." It is more like, "Adam gave away his strength" or, "my flesh the weasel did it." It is not even "the devil made me do it," but "my poser-/false self made me do it." Where is God in this picture besides sitting on the therapy couch?

Is Your Heart Good?

"You have a new heart. . .your heart is good, and sin is not the deepest thing about you" (Eldredge 134, 144), Eldredge says. To help prove the point he tells us, God has never told anyone to crucify their hearts or to "kill the true man within us" with its "deep desires for battle, adventure, and a beauty to win" (145). But these statements are confusing on three counts.

First, they cause us to think that the "true self" is without sin. The apostle John says in 1 John 1:8, "If we say that we have no sin, we deceive ourselves, and the truth is not in us." The apostle John is strongly affirming that every born-again Christian sins and anyone who denies this fact is self-deceived. To claim as Eldredge does that one's true and good heart is exempt from sin, and that the sin issue is with the poser-/false self, is misleading, and confusing theology.

Secondly, Eldredge downplays the nature of sin in man. It is now more of a nuisance than the deadly poison revealed in Scripture. But to diminish the nature of sin and its potential in the heart of man is to erode the doctrine of sanctification.

Thirdly, our writer is equating the desires of masculinity and femininity with our new nature in Christ. When he says God never told us to kill the true man within us with his deep desires, Eldredge is implying that the true man is pristine in nature and good. Though it is true that the Bible teaches that men and women are made in God's image, it is equally as true that we are, in all our creaturely ways (including our passions and desires), distorted, twisted, and rebellious. That would include Eldredge's archetypes of adventure, battle, and a beauty to win. These universal traits, though true and exciting for men, are also distorted by sin. They only become valuable when they are sanctified and put in the service of King Jesus.

8

HEALING THE WOUND
OR REPENTANCE?

"God is fiercely committed to you, to the restoration and release of your masculine heart. But a wound that goes unacknowledged and unwept is a wound that cannot heal" (Eldredge 106). First, God is not revealed in Scripture as having a purpose to restore and release your masculine heart. That is not a biblical doctrine. His expressed will is that we would be conformed into the image of Christ, which is moral and spiritual. Healing and woundedness, and masculinity are secondary issues at best.

Secondly, the statement that, "A wound that goes unacknowledged and unwept is a wound that cannot heal" is a wise saying in reference to inner healing but not in salvation. Salvation is first moral before it is therapeutic. This is the psychologizing of the biblical doctrine of salvation. Removing the therapeutic spin and adding a moral framework would cause this statement to read thus: "A sin unacknowledged and unwept is a sin that cannot be forgiven."

It's Still Not My Fault

Using the movie *Good Will Hunting* as a parable of wisdom, Eldredge makes the case that a person can take responsibility for a wound that is really not his/her fault. The character in the movie is Will Hunting, a young man who has a false self of violence born out of a father wound (Eldredge 124). As Will gets in trouble he ends up with a psychologist (Robin Williams) who nourishes Will with the masculine love he has never had. Eldredge reminds us that this is the beginning of Will's initiation into manhood. After Will gets in touch with his pain and father wound, the psychologist holds up his file and tells him, "It's not your fault." This is the concept Eldredge continually leads his readers, "It's not your fault" (125). Once again this book does a great disfavor to its readers. It casts a shadow over their responsibility for sin.

Today, many in the church have lost their Christ-centeredness because of this kind of psychologizing of Scripture. Subtly, their Christianity has become gutless with no responsibility to live righteously. Life has been reduced to inward feelings, woundedness, and the heart. I will say it again. These are not the great themes of the Bible. Jesus Christ is the great theme. To get these mixed up, is to substitute man for God.

Jesus, Take Me Into My Wound

Wild at Heart is all about men and their wounds. It is about relieving them of their conviction of sin, the sin that should be driving them to brokenness and deep repentance of their rebellion against God. Eldredge is giving men permission to be comfortable where they are by telling them they are victims, that it is not their fault, and that God receives them just as they are. I don't minimize the pain and wounds that people have. They are real and hurtful. What is troubling is placing man and his healing at the center of life rather than God.

The primary message of the gospel is not about inner healing, but it is a message of righteousness and escaping the wrath of God to come. It should not be "Jesus take me into my wound" as Eldredge claims, but "Jesus forgive me of my sins" as the Bible claims.

Salvation is Not Inner Healing

The central message of the Bible according to Eldredge is Luke 4:18 (Isaiah 61:1). Here he says "Christ comes to restore and release you, your soul, the true you" (Eldredge 129). Eldredge psychologizes these verses and in so doing converts them into a therapeutic doctrine of salvation through inner healing. We grieve our wounds—"Daddy didn't give me toy guns for Christmas, boo hoo."

Though healing is by definition included in salvation, those who heard Jesus expound (Isaiah 61) understood him to be announcing the coming of the Kingdom reign of God. This text is first a political statement announcing real debt forgiveness to the poor, release for those in jail, and a reference to the social policies of the year of Jubilee (Deuteronomy 15, Leviticus 25). At the same time, in the context of the New Testament, it is the announcement of the glorious gospel about to be actualized. The debt of sin is about to be dealt with by the sacrifice of Christ. The captives are about to be truly liberated. But Eldredge personalizes the Kingdom's impact, rendering it a gospel of inner healing.

A Man's Addictions—Refusing His Strength?

Eldredge gives an example of a man named Carl who had a sexual weakness with ladies. The whole sexual struggle was not so much sin, Eldredge says, but a battle for his strength

(Eldredge 147). Eldredge tells us that a man's addictions are the result of his refusing his strength (149). Men would be free if they would let their strength arrive. Yet what does this mean? This coded psychobabble is evasive.

Eldredge does say Carl confessed his sin; that, I can understand. But then he says Carl, through prayer, cleansed his strength; that, I don't understand. What is it that was cleansed and what was it cleansed from? What does it mean to cleanse your strength? Is this a sanctification of one's testosterone? Cleansing your strength seems a far cry from, "Let us cleanse ourselves from all filthiness of the flesh and spirit, perfecting holiness in the fear of God" (2 Corinthians 7:1).

9

ELDREDGE AND...

The Testimonies of Men

But what about all the testimonies of men who say the book has really helped them? No doubt some may have that testimony. Nevertheless, pragmatism (what works) doesn't make something biblically true or sound in doctrine. Because it works doesn't mean it is true.

This book surely rings the masculine "bell" as few books have. It draws men right into themselves by touching the things that touch men. As men read that they have permission to be free and to passionately pursue adventure, battle, and the golden haired woman, something inside of them says "Yeah!" After all, what man couldn't identify with climbing Mount Everest, storming the WW II beaches of Omaha, or rescuing a distressed maiden? Like Bly, Eldredge has touched traits common to men as well as their pains, desires, and needs. He goes to great lengths to draw them into identifying with these themes through stories and his own self-disclosure.

In literature, the practice of self-disclosure is often a common therapeutic technique that is used to invite readers into the inner experiences of the writer. It gives the impression that the writer (therapist) has experienced inner fears, pain, and thoughts similar to that of the reader. This also gives the impression that the writer is both approachable and knowledgeable about the inner life. He or she appears to have authority.

Yet, just because people identify with the elements of the masculine nature and its passion, doesn't mean those things are biblically sound. From a therapeutic worldview it does, but not from a biblical worldview.

The sad thing is that many men, who themselves are often disoriented for lack of a solid biblical base, hook into this message thinking it to be true because it feels right and seems to work. They mistake their positive experiences (it feels so right) as being the proof of the teaching. But nothing could be further from the truth. The only compass for navigating our spiritual life is the Scriptures. When we follow our natural wisdom and feelings we will plunge into deception.

Divorce

In my opinion, it is alarming when an author of a book that is suppose to teach men, reveals his own whelms of anger in which he confesses the thought of divorcing his wife (Eldredge 152). It is not that I have a problem with the openness and transparency of the statement. I just think it is not becoming of one who teaches others about marriage and manhood. Of course, maybe I am just out of touch.

By the time he writes the closing chapters, he again confesses that in a moment of conflict with his wife Stasi, he was tired of fighting for their marriage. Being tempted to go to a bar for relief of the pain and disappointment in his heart, he prays and hears the Lord tell him to go dance with his wife (Eldredge 194, 195). Yet again, for a man who is teaching other men how they should live and where the answers are, I would expect more maturity.

Dangerous Men

Eldredge affirms that men need to have relationships but not the accountability type. That is, well, '"old school" according to Eldredge. What we need are fellow warriors, a band of brothers, to watch our backs. "The whole crisis in masculinity today has come because we no longer have a warrior culture, a place for men to learn to fight like men. We don't need a meeting of really nice guys, we need a gathering of really dangerous men" (Eldredge 175). So what is this man talking about? I guess I am confused because I keep running the content of this book through a biblical grid. Eldredge obviously has some other kind of grid—a quasi-psycho/spiritual one.

Listen, the only dangerous men I know of are those who have yielded themselves to be vessels of the Holy Spirit. The book of Acts is about a band of brothers who were not nice guys, they were really dangerous. What is Eldredge's idea of a gathering of really dangerous men? Are they filled with the Holy Spirit? Is the place shaken when they pray? Do they go into the world and preach the gospel, and do they heal the sick and cast out devils? No, his idea of dangerous is fly-fishing, standing up for your rights, and climbing a mountain. His is a truly Americanized gospel.

"Ache" Theology?

Eldredge tells us that Adam chose Eve over God, and Eve took the place of God in a man's life (Eldredge115). From this premise we are told men are aching for what they know not. Supposedly it is for God, but they have become confused and substituted the woman in His place because she is the closest thing to God as the pinnacle of creation.

Eldredge says this ache is the reason men struggle with sexual issues. They are lonely, beat up, and longing for comfort and so turn to whatever can quench their thirst and relieve their ache. They are to be pitied because they are only trying to satisfy their deep need for God (Eldredge 116, 117). But the Scripture looks at this quite differently.

First, man's deepest desire is not for union with God. The Scripture says, "There is none that understandeth, there is none that seeketh after God" (Romans 3:11). Still Eldredge follows the unbiblical thought of Manning: "The deepest desire of our hearts is for union with God" (Eldredge 119). These kinds of assumptions are spurious.

Secondly, the Bible does not say woman is the pinnacle of creation, just the opposite. The Bible says Eve (the woman) was made subordinate to man and was not made the pinnacle of creation: "Nor was man created for the woman, but woman for the man" (1 Corinthians 11:9). Also, the Scripture says man was made to be the glory of the woman, and Christ is the glory of the man. All this ache theology is just more of this book's psycho- babble.

With this kind of underlying theology, it is very important that the reader of *Wild at Heart* consider the source. Remember also, just because Eldredge is a Christian doesn't mean his book is. Because of Bly, Lee, Manning, and a whole framework of anti-Christian principles, this book is dangerously deceptive. Yes, it is charming and insightful as relating to aspects of human nature, but it is equally seductive, cunning and very deceptive, especially in this day of a famine of sound doctrine.

The superficial Christian community is more than eager to gobble this stuff up, but this seemingly delightful dish contains deadly poison.

Mother Teresa or *Braveheart*?

In man's search for his strength, to tell him that God is his father is bogus. God, according to Eldredge, is weak or unrelated from most men's point of view. "Be honest" Eldredge says, "Isn't your idea of Jesus that he was soft?" And isn't this what the church projects on men, "Be nice, a kind of Mother Teresa" (Eldredge 22)?

Some churches may project such an image, but I know this, the Bible points men more toward the character of someone like Mother Teresa in her selflessness than ever toward *Braveheart's* William Wallace in his self-will. Mother Teresa lived moral virtue of selfless serving. In her humility she was a rugged defender of the poorest of the poor. But what of this movie character Wallace? He is representative of a macho mania man. To compare her to an earthy macho character (like she needs to get a real life), should be an embarrassment to Eldredge. But he tells us that men relate to Wallace, and this myth model of warrior/leader is more indicative of the kind of man Jesus was. Yet the biblical description of Jesus is not one of a '"cool macho dude." Jesus described himself in very contrary terms, "For I am gentle and lowly in heart" (Matthew 11:29).

Initiation into Manhood

Eldredge tells us that men need to be initiated into manhood. He says the church would like to think it has done this but it has only invited men into what is moral, which he says is "pitifully insufficient and never the point" (Eldredge 101). (This is a pitiful statement in my estimation.)

First, the church does not have the mandate to initiate men into masculinity. That is not its calling. The church does have the mandate to invite men and women into taking up their crosses and following Jesus. This is an invitation into life, which when lived, will produce a biblical masculinity or femininity that does not deny the moral, but lives it.

So contrary to *Wild at Heart*, the answers are not in secular versions of manhood, but in being born again in Christ, which is always moral. Eldredge wants to add something to Christianity, but it is earthy and lacking in power. He should be inviting men and women to repent and serve the Lord with their whole hearts. He should be initiating them into a life of selflessness for the gospel and into being baptized in the Holy Spirit. He should be leading them into the Word of God to find the answers to who they are, and what they are to be. For only in God will one find true adventure, true battle, and a true beauty to win. Only there will one find the true answers of life and a real impetus for manhood. That's because Christ and His Word are sufficient for all things that pertain to life and godliness, and be assured, biblical masculinity will be godly.

10

Conclusion

....

ASKING THE WRONG QUESTIONS

....

Men are afraid, afraid they will be found out. They are haunted by the question, "Am I really a man? Have I got what it takes . . . when it counts?" In response to this, men fake having it together when in reality they don't. The lack of transparency and honesty among men, especially Christian men, proves the point (Eldredge 54), according to Eldredge.

He also says church is especially a '"poser" kind of place where men need to come out from behind their fears and stand up—stand up to their pastor (Eldredge 55, 56). Yet as real as some of these questions and observations may be, they are not the true questions. They do not represent biblical questions about the nature and need of man. If you don't ask the right question, how can you get the right answer?

"Am I really a man? Have I got what it takes . . . when it counts?" It isn't as if these are not legitimate questions of confidence and identity, which men wrestle with. It is just that they are not central to godliness.

From a biblical view, a real man is one who denies himself and follows Jesus as Lord embracing the responsibilities to live the life of Christ. For instance, in marriage the Bible says a Christian man is to lay his life down for his wife as Christ did for the church. He is to turn away from ungodliness. A man who doesn't provide for his family is an infidel and has denied the faith. The Bible says not one word about stirring yourself up in masculine passions but a lot about living righteously—devotedly.

And when a man asks, "Have I got what it takes?", I want to ask, is this a category of biblical masculinity? If it is, Paul the apostle has the answer. He said, "Within me dwells no good thing," and "When I am weak then I am strong." This is of course the antithesis of Eldredge's question. Instead of asking ridiculous questions like "Have I got what it takes?", or "Am I powerful?", we should be asking more classical questions such as, "Who do you love?" (Augustine) and "Who will you serve?" (Jesus). This is how the Bible spells out manhood.

Eldredge Doesn't Know the Real Problem

Eldredge invites men to come alive and to find their great battle, adventure, and beauty by rediscovering their lost masculinity and healing their masculine soul. But the problem is not where Eldredge thinks it is. Though he gives an astute description of tired, bored men, his answers cannot succeed. The reason is that he does not know the real problem, which is a failure in appropriating the life of Christ. He thinks healing the father wound and releasing the strength of lost spiritual masculinity is the cure, but it is not.

There is a disease more fundamental. It is the sickness of men and women not having been wholly converted to Christ. They may call themselves Christians, but nothing in them makes them alive, *really* come alive. The reason is they have not come to the Lord on His terms in deep repentance.

The church is full of dead-wood today because it has invited people to a gospel void of a command to repentant and be filled with the Holy Spirit. Men and women, boys and girls have not been shown their own depravity nor their sin against a Holy God. Instead they have been led to a shallow and powerless confession of Christ, or to a therapeutic repentance made up of confessing one's hurts. Either way the results are the same: people naming the name of Christ but who are helpless to depart from iniquity. And so they are bored and tired and the commands of God are burdensome.

Pop-Tart Psychology

On the contrary Eldredge concerns himself and his readers with tasty Pop-Tart psychological concepts that have no power to do anything other than create self-absorption. Because Eldredge doesn't understand the real issues, he can't provide real answers. This is why he says nothing about repentance toward God, or being filled with the Spirit of God. He directs no one to Scripture nor challenges anyone to deny ungodliness and worldly lusts. Instead, he brings what he projects as a better frame of reference—Bly, archetypes, *Braveheart*, the father wound, your heart is good, fly-fishing, and deep masculinity.

However, all of this is a far cry from the experiences of those in the Bible. The men and women of the book of Acts had no time to sink into their wounds with Jesus. They were ablaze with the love of God and went forth into the adventure and battle of winning the world to Christ. They were not gazing inward while parked at a pub or backpacking. Their worldview was moral and not therapeutic. They went forth as real men and women winning the day in the power of a Spirit-filled life.

When they preached, hearts were cut. When they prayed, the place was shaken. How different this picture is, from what is painted on the therapy couch of John Eldredge's *Wild at Heart*.

END NOTES

1. John Eldredge, *Wild at Heart: Discovering the Secret of a Man's Soul* (Thomas Nelson Publishers, 2001).

2. An author, counselor and lecturer, John Eldredge was a writer and speaker for *Focus on the Family* for more than twelve years. He received his undergraduate degree in theater from California State Polytechnic University and worked as an actor and director in Los Angeles for ten years. He received his masters degree in counseling from Colorado Christian University, under the direction of Drs. Larry Crabb and Dan Allender.

3. Os Guinness, *No God But God: Breaking with the Idols of Our Age*, (Chicago, IL: Moody Press, 1992), 130. "The overall story of pastoral care in the United States has been summed up as the shift from salvation to self-realization, made up of smaller shifts from self-denial to self-love to self-mastery, and finally to self-realization. The victory of the therapeutic over theology is

therefore nothing less than the secularization and replacement of salvation." —Os Guinness

4. I define psycho-spiritual as some idea of psychology that is claimed as spiritual. Eldredge clearly equates the desires of the masculine heart as a kind of spiritual truth: "Adventure is a deeply spiritual longing written into the soul of man" (Eldredge 5), and there "are three desires I find written so deeply into my heart I know now I can no longer disregard them without losing my soul" (9).

5. David F. Wells, *God in the Wasteland*, (Grand Rapids, Michigan: W. B. Eerdmans, 1994), 115.

6. John Eldredge Web site mission statement. (http:// www.ransomedheart.com)

7. Michael Scott Horton, ed., *Power Religion: The Selling Out of the Evangelical Church?* (Chicago, IL: Moody, 1992). Michael Horton says: "But what we see today in so much of the literature and preaching of Christian pop psychology is not integration of biblical-theological and natural-scientific knowledge, but a replacement of biblical views of humans, God, and salvation with purely secular notions, baptized with non-contextual verses from the Bible."

8. Natural theology is the effort to gain knowledge of God from reason and nature. I have thought that maybe *Wild at Heart* should be given credit as an effort to derive a model of masculinity from a kind of natural theology. Eldredge says he drew much of his insights from talking with many, many men and women, from boyhood dreams, from literature, fly-fishing,

poetry, myth, movies, and nature (Eldredge 128). And it is these insights that he casts as deep spiritual truths and upon which he builds his model of masculinity. Though his observations may tell us something of the natural traits of men and women, they don't give us a biblical picture. What they do give is a distortion. A picture of human nature that fails to take into account the utter depravity of man, and a distorted view of God that is wholly man-centered. This supposed natural theology, if it can be called that, with man as its center, is certainly destined to fall short. It can rise no higher than its basic premise—man.

9. The depravity of man is the Orthodox Christian doctrine, which says all have sinned and it is the nature of man. Paul put it this way, "within me dwells no good thing." Eldredge is confusing this with the implied thought that something good is really in the deep heart of man.

10. St. Thomas Aquinas, *Summa Theologica*. Section I, Orgins End 93, part6. (http://www.newadvent.org/summa/109306.htm)

Appendix 1

UNDERSTANDING THE
THERAPEUTIC WORLD

Western culture has become a culture of the therapeutic, where life is personalized and reduced to feelings, self-actualization, and a quest for personal healing. This psychological view of living has almost completely marginalized the moral worldview that previously dominated our way of life.

The moral view, with its dual emphasis on the inward state of character and virtue, and its outward duty of responsibility, has been discounted in favor of self and its internal elusive feelings.

In the therapeutic world, moral character qualities like discipline, honesty, dutiful, and faithfulness, are replaced by one's own personal feelings and persuasions. And the more personal something is perceived to be, the more authority is ascribed to it. Whatever feels most "real" therefore trumps everything else, including morals.

This is because in a psychologized world, where feelings and preferences are the guiding lights, no moral norms are at the center of living. Hence, very little is binding on self or others. Everything is basically relative. It is an immoral world.

Yet to the contrary, a biblical worldview has character and moral norms at its center. Private and public preferences are not left to their own personal whims but are instead subjugated to the moral center of life. And the center of morality is the holiness of God, which is binding on all.

Under the influence of a therapeutic worldview, society has gone on a great quest for wholeness, release from pain, self-realization, and a new image. Almost all marketing today is either about something that will improve one's status, give release from pain, or fulfill some desire. And this view is not totally secular; it has also penetrated the church as the therapeutic gospel.

David Wells comments, in a psychologized culture there is a deep need for relational experience but a dis-*ease* with what is moral. "This carries over into the church as an infatuation with the love of God and an embarrassment at his holiness." We think of God more like a therapist who is calling out our knowledge of ourselves while passing judgment on none of it.

This disposition leads us to believe our faith is wholly relational and internal. We imagine the great purposes of life are psychological rather than moral. We think that the great purposes of life are realized in the improvement of our own private inner disposition. The therapeutic has overshadowed the moral even in the church.

The truth is, the Bible never promises anyone a life free of stresses, pains, and ambiguities. [It does not offer psychological wholeness as its first priority though it produces it.] There must be a recovery of the idea that being made in God's image, we are fundamentally immoral beings, not consumers, that the

Appendix 1

satisfaction of our psychological needs pales in significance when compared with the enduring value of doing what is right.

David F. Wells, *God in the Wasteland*, (Grand Rapids, Michigan: W. B. Eerdmans, 1994), 114, 115.

Uncovering Wild at Heart

Appendix 2

....

A HISTORY OF BLY AND THE
MYTHOPOETIC MEN'S MOVEMENT

....

Like most mythopoetic teachers, Bly makes use of Jung's theory of archetypes, arguing that within each man there are numerous archetypes that will influence behavior and attitudes, some in healthy ways and some in violent and unhealthy ways. These archetypes include the Wild Man, the King, the Trickster, the Lover, and the Warrior. Masculinity is the product of these deep psychological scripts.

For Bly, there have been distinct historical forms of masculinity. The 1950s male was the organization man, the 1960s and early 1970s male was an angry macho warrior, the late 1970's and 1980s male was a soft [nice guy], feminized man. Through long-term historical shifts, collective rituals of manhood have disintegrated [see this concept in Eldredge 67], and father-son solidarity is now absent, damaged by changes in the organization of work that were apart of the Industrial

Revolution [the result of modernity (see Eldredge 6)]. Masculinity is currently unhealthy and spiritually limiting.

Men must therefore descend into their spirits, into the "deep masculine," and make contact with an important archetype — the Wild Man. Bly retells the Grimm Brothers fairytale *Iron Hans* as *Iron John* to introduce the Wild Man. In this interpretation, personal growth begins with this spiritual discovery, achieved through participation in rituals, myths, and storytelling.

The concept of the Wild Man represents the wild and vigorous nature of man that has been suppressed in modern males, and that we need to rediscover to break out of our spiritual malaise. If this part of masculinity is properly integrated into the male psyche, it will be positive and creative.

The Wild Man is a spontaneous, forceful, primal being. The Wild Man represents the "nourishing and spiritually radiant energy" of the "deep masculine." Bly has in mind the kind of energy that involves "forceful action undertaken, not without compassion, but with resolve." Wild men are not hostile and aggressive, but show a steady resolve to know and defend what they love.

Bly distinguishes between the Wild Man and the Savage Man, who is hostile, insensitive, and full of rage. The Savage Man has repressed his basic nature, ignored his hurts, and is in many ways the antithesis of the Wild Man.

In the ideal world of Bly's mythopoetic men, the animal nature of man is acknowledged and embraced; the warrior is noble and never savage; the king is wise and sensitive; the poet and shaman are honored; the father and son are loving mentor and pupil; all emotion is acknowledged.

Bly's exhortation for a return to the Wild Man is based partly on the argument that the 1960s and 70s were characterized by the "soft male"— men who have abandoned their "masculine energy" [strengthen according to Eldredge], as a response to the questioning of masculinity by feminists in particular. "Soft males" lack initiative and strength, are confused about their identity, and unable to relate to their masculinity. Bly therefore preaches that men rediscover and express their energy and strength, their ability to shout and say what they want" [Eldredge tells men to stand up to the woman, stand up to the pastor, and say what you want (Eldredge 150, 151, 177)].

Michael Flood—used by permission.

Appendix 3

······································

WHAT IS GRACE?

······································

There is a fatal error in our understanding of the grace of God. Grace has come to be portrayed as a cover-up for whatever ails us, a justification for self-seeking and disobedient life-styles. The saying, "I am covered by grace" is the common response to any suggestion of personal responsibility to walk in obedience and holiness. The mere mention of obedience is often considered to be an attack on grace and is branded immediately as a work of legalism. We are reminded that salvation is the free gift of God, and that it is by grace, and not works. Though this latter statement is true, it is not the whole truth. Consider these words from the Bible:

> "For the grace of God that brings salvation has appeared to all men, teaching us that, denying ungodliness and worldly lusts, we should live soberly, righteously, and godly in this present age." (Titus 2:11-12)

What must become clear is that the grace of God is the essence of the power of God to enable Christians to live a life of holiness as well as being a provision for sinfulness.

The writer of Hebrews exhorts, "let us have grace, by which we may serve God acceptably with reverence and godly fear" (Hebrews 12:28). Here again, grace is not defined as an all-purpose covering for failure, but a force that enables us to serve God acceptably with godliness.

Paul exhorts the Corinthian church to, "not receive the grace of God in vain" (2 Corinthians 6:1). To receive something in vain would be not to use its potential; like receiving a parachute in a failing airplane. That parachute would be your salvation but if you did not deploy it, you would have received it in vain. In the same way, to receive God's grace in vain would mean that he has given the power to walk free and to live in holiness but it was neglected and like the parachute, never deployed.

Grace that is received in vain results in an unchanged life in regards to impurities and lusts of the world.

The fruit of holiness is the proof of living in the true grace of God.

INDEX

Index

Index

Index

Index

Index

Index

Index

Meet Tom Griner

 **Tom Griner** is a seasoned pastor and missionary evangelist who has been in ministry for over thirty years.

He is the founder and president of Father's Heart International (www.fhafrica.org), an organization dedicated to hunger relief of starving children, as well as church planting through support of African national pastors.

Griner earned a bachelor of science from Oral Roberts University in 1973, a master of divinity from Anaheim School of Theology in 1978, and a doctor of ministry from Oral Roberts University in 1997.

He is the author of: *Wounded Continent: Partnering with the African Church to save the dying;* and *Word of Knowledge: How to Minister in Revelation.*

Dr. Griner is married to Kathie, his wife of 27 years. They have three daughters, Danielle, Bethany, and Lacy. They live in Nevada.